Nurturing Myself

Interactive Journal for Women

5 Ways to Nurture Yourself in 5 Minutes or Less

by

Jean S. Wittig

For Elaine

Best Wishes

Jean

Illustrations by Roger Conover

Open Door Publications

Nurturing Nellie's
Interactive Journal for Women
5 Ways to Nurture Yourself in 5 Minutes or Less

© 2009 Jean S. Wittig
www.JeanWittig.com

Published by:
Open Door Publications
27 Carla Way
Lawrenceville, NJ 08648

Illustrations by Roger Conover

Cover & Interior Design by Synectic Studio
www.synecticstudio.com

ISBN: 978-0-9789792-5-9

This publication is designed to provide inspiration only.
It is purchased or otherwise transferred with the understanding
that this is not a rendering of professional services or advice
by the author, publisher, editor, and illustrator.
You are advised to consult your own mental health or
other professional as needed.

I lovingly dedicate this book to my sister, Anne.

Acknowledgements

A special thank you to all my teachers, especially Anne S. Doody, the Reverend Annie Greenleaf, Sharon Wilson, Sherry Hudson and Dave Ellis. What I learned from all of you has made it possible for me to create Nurturing Nellie and to become Nurturing Nellie for myself.

Many thanks to Roger Conover whose artistic talent brought Nurturing Nellie to life, and to Karen Hodges Miller for carrying me through the entire process of writing and publishing this book.

Appreciation and love go out to my family for supporting me throughout the many months I spent working on this book: my husband Paul, and my children Lynda and Jamie Dawson, Barbara Wittig and Joanna Wittig.

Table of Contents

Introduction 9

An Interview with Nurturing Nellie ....…................ 12

MESSAGE 1:   Shower with one minute of self-love daily 15

Journal of Experiences for Message 1 22

MESSAGE 2:   Set simple, well-timed intentions
              that nurture YOU! 29

Journal of Experiences for Message 2 38

MESSAGE 3:   Find inspiration to feed your soul
              in any given moment ....…... 45

Journal of Experiences for Message 3 52

MESSAGE 4:   Replace multi-tasking with mindfulness ....…... 59

Journal of Experiences for Message 4 64

MESSAGE 5:   Document your attitude of gratitude
              as a gift to yourself 71

Journal of Experiences for Message 5 78

Summary 85

Count Your Blessings Gratitude Journal 87

Bibliography 126

Introduction

Nurturing Nellie™, the delightful character on the cover, was created as a rendering of my interpretation of the words, "Love thy neighbor as thyself." To me, the phrase implies: love and take care of others *in the same way* you love and take care of yourself, *not more than* and *not less than* yourself. Yet many of us were raised to believe that it is selfish or arrogant to love ourselves, and more virtuous to show love to others first.

This book was born out of my personal journey of growth and self-discovery and my work with women since 1989. As a life-long learner, a teacher, and my roles as both participant and leader with spirituality circles, I have learned ways to live more joyfully and *give* more joyfully as I became more like the character of Nellie. The many women I have met and worked with have inspired me to create this interactive journal; to reach out to the woman who always nurtures and gives to others, and feels guilty for wanting time for herself.

What's valuable about **5 Ways to Nurture Yourself in 5 Minutes or Less** is that the five messages, and the cartoons that accompany them, are geared toward raising awareness and shifting thinking to increase emotional energy and personal well-being within the time frame of simple daily situations. You can be empowered to feel better in the moment and bring out your best without waiting until you can take a walk or schedule time away. For example, the ripple effect of creating a well-timed inspiring intention statement for yourself, as you begin a confrontational conversation at home or at work, (Message 2) can reach far beyond your highest expectation, and come back to nurture you in ways you never anticipated.

Nurturing Nellie's Interactive Journal for Women grew out of one of my favorite topics for self-reflection and discussion: *"giving and receiving."* We often begin a discussion in women's groups by asking, "Do you agree with this statement: *it is better to give than to receive."*

There are always many perspectives to listen to, but over the years I have noticed that many women say it is easy for them to give while it is difficult for them to receive. Some women even find it uncomfortable just receiving a simple compliment, or feel guilty when relaxing or doing something for themselves.

Yet giving and receiving follow a natural law of rhythm. The tides go in and the tides go out. Trees lose their leaves and new ones appear. When a woman tells me she is very happy to give a compliment but reluctant to receive one, I say, "That's like only breathing out! What happens when you don't breathe in?"

Many of us understand first-hand that patterns of giving to others without replenishing ourselves can result in stress, burn-out, and resentment - a less than healthy state of being. If you are a woman who always gives to others first and you're simply worn out from doing so, then this book is for YOU!

The energy we offer others is key. We know from scientific research that all matter is energy and everything has a vibrational frequency, even our attitudes. If our attitude is one of resentment or burn-out from always putting others first, we produce a lower energetic output. When we raise our awareness and increase our frequency to higher attitudes of peace, joy and love, then that is what we radiate out to others, and by the law of attraction - we reap what we sow - that is what comes back to us in return.

Nellie's five "messages" or chapters are presented as an interactive journal to give you the opportunity to learn new skills, develop new patterns of thinking, and record reflections of your journey to enhanced well-being via the paths of self-care, self-love, and self-nurturing. Expressing our inner thoughts through journaling is an excellent way to gain clarity, amplify the learning experience, and support ourselves through the process of experiencing a discovery or a re-discovery in each of the five chapters.

Each chapter or "message" stands by itself and the messages can be read in any order. In addition to the guided journaling within each chapter, the second part of this book contains a free-form journal called the **Count Your Blessings Gratitude Journal** which we hope you will use as often as you can to record positive aspects of daily situations, gratitude for the blessings in your life, big and small, and simple musings or reflections on your daily life.

I hope you take pleasure in using the journaling opportunities as you move through each of Nellie's messages, and other times throughout your busy life.

While you may at first be turning to Nurturing Nellie to guide you through new experiences, it is my sincere hope that each one of you will become a Nurturing Nellie during this process! Most importantly, remember to **be gentle with yourself.** Just as you give the best care that you can to others, you also deserve to give the best care to YOURSELF!

Jean S. Wittig

An Interview with Nurturing Nellie

Q: Let's start by asking, how did you get your name?

A: Well, at first I was always taking care of everybody and every...*thing* else. My family and friends, my plants, my pets....

Q: Isn't that pretty normal?

A: Sure, I was nurturing THEM, but I wasn't taking care of ME enough! I was getting worn out. And I was feeling guilty doing things just for me.

Q: So what happened?

A: I took a vacation and on the airplane, they said, if there's an emergency and the oxygen masks come down, "put YOURS on first, then help others." THAT really made me think about how I see things!

Q: And that changed things?

A: It was the START of changing things. I also began to learn about myself more. It was a huge ... s-t-r-e-t-c-h for me. *Look at my right arm... I really stretched out of my comfort zone!* I began to understand more about the body-mind-spirit connection and how paying attention to all three can play a big part in my well-being. I started learning how to give to myself... nurturing myself more ... and learning more about forgiveness and self-acceptance. It really makes a big difference. Now, everybody calls me Nurturing Nellie because they see me the way this picture looks ... giving to myself, as well as to everyone else.

Q: So tell me, what IS in that watering can above your head?

A: Lots of things, like self-love, being open to new ideas, gratitude, and other wonderful things that nourish my spirit. If you have some time now, I can tell you five ways I like to give to myself without feeling guilty or selfish.

Q: I DO have time now, but first tell me more about not feeling guilty.

A: That took a little time to evolve, but less than I thought it would. When I finally realized that I can honor others better and give to them more joyfully when I have honored MYSELF first ... that really felt good!! I can live with that!

Q: We're all so busy these days. How do you find time for yourself?

A: Sometimes I dedicate a specific time to meditate, spend an afternoon with a friend, get a massage, or just sit and read for an hour... but I've learned five ways to nurture myself by simply shifting my thinking or attitude in only a few moments, and the results can last all day. Now that I've been changing my thinking daily, those five principles have become habits, and I feel a lot better in general.

As you listen to me describe these new habits, you may decide to put them into practice yourself. If you DO decide to make some changes, remember to BE GENTLE WITH YOURSELF along the way!

Message 1: _____

Shower with one minute of self-love daily

When I look in the mirror each morning, I lovingly
greet the person in the reflection. "Good Morning.
I love you Nellie. I approve of you.
I accept you as a unique person."
- Nurturing Nellie

When you're in front of the mirror each morning, how do you treat the image you see in the reflection?

With love and kindness? Or with a put down and old messages from the past?

With gentle acceptance of who you are and what you see? Or with a judgment that you're "not enough" and an unrealistic wish to be something different?

Certainly a mirror can be a positive force during our day and alert us to the fact that we need to comb our hair, adjust our outfit, or brush that last bit of green veggie out of our teeth. These simple acts of grooming are straightforward responses to situations that can help us put our best foot forward as we go out into the world.

Yet many women look at the figure in the mirror and begin to express disapproval in some form of "I'm not good enough."

Throughout the day, thoughts of not being enough, not doing enough, making a mistake, or doing something "wrong" can drag us down.

"How stupid of me to forget my cell-phone. What's wrong with me that I can't find my keys? How could I have made such a dumb comment?"

Perhaps criticism is what you've lived with in the past, from others and even from yourself. And those statements of disapproval are still living in your mind. But the past is just that – past, done, over. You have the capacity to reject past statements, release the self-criticism and choose a new response to each situation. A habitual critical response from you can be replaced with a loving response, one that is a simple statement of fact, curiosity, forgiveness or an intention statement.

The condemnation of *"How stupid of me to forget my cell phone,"* can be extinguished with a statement of fact and curiosity.

"Oops! I didn't bring my cell phone. I wonder what I can do about that?"

The disapproval in the statement, *"What's wrong with me that I can't find my keys. I'm such a jerk,"* can be extinguished with acceptance, love, and an intention statement. (More details about intention statements in Message 2.)

"Even though I can't find my keys right now, I love me. I intend to joyfully take the spare key to get two duplicates made just for hectic times like this."

The self-blame in the statement, *"How could I have made such a dumb comment. I'm always saying the wrong thing,"* can be extinguished with forgiveness and an intention statement.

"I forgive myself for making that insensitive comment and I intend to write a note of apology."

"I learned that self-love works from the inside with self-approval, self-acceptance, and self-forgiveness. No one else can give me those inner feelings."

Love, Nellie

Nellie's loving message in action

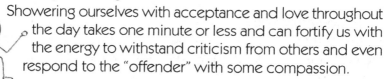

Showering ourselves with acceptance and love throughout the day takes one minute or less and can fortify us with the energy to withstand criticism from others and even respond to the "offender" with some compassion.

When we time ourselves with a full minute of loving and positive self-talk it may seem silly at first. With practice, it begins to feel normal.

When is a good time to shower with self-love and acceptance?

- ❧ When you look in the mirror – say "I love you" to yourself
- ❧ When you take a shower – imagine lots of love in the streams of warm water
- ❧ Each time you hear a critical voice in your head
- ❧ Whenever you hear a put down from someone else

Ideas for showering with self-love and acceptance

☑ For one minute, play the rapid-fire game *"What I like about me is…"* Acknowledge even the most mundane things. If nothing comes to mind immediately, simply say, "everything." It goes something like this:

What I like about me is – I brush my teeth
What I like about me is – I'm a good driver
What I like about me is – uhh, uhh, everything
What I like about me is – I'm trustworthy

What I like about me is – I'm reading this book
What I like about me is – I'm learning something
What I like about me is – I'm creative

☑ In lieu of this verbal exercise, you might choose to record something in the Count Your Blessings Gratitude Journal, such as:

❥ *I'm grateful for the water and toothpaste to brush my teeth.*
❥ *What's positive today is that I drove several places and arrived safely.*

☑ Deliberately notice any self-condemnation in your thoughts or self-talk. Then become even more of a critic. Decide whether the statement is true - something that truly warrants attention - or is it a habitual self-criticism that needs to be extinguished.

Example: You forgot about a dentist appointment you've waited weeks for, because of a hectic schedule. You begin to berate yourself, and feel guilty or incompetent.

Instead of speaking harshly to yourself be gentle and choose a new language pattern.

❥ statement of fact: *"Yikes, my time just got away from me!"*

❥ self-forgiveness: *"I forgive myself for this and for not acting the way I wanted to act."*

❥ curiosity: *"I wonder when I can re-schedule?"*

❥ intention statement: *"I intend to apologize to the dentist for missing my appointment and resolve to become better organized with my time and appointment book so this doesn't happen again."*

Practice Lovingly – Be gentle with yourself

List two habitual situations when you typically criticize yourself and write a more loving statement that's easy to extinguish the criticism.

1. Statement of self-criticism _____

_____

   Statement of self-love and acceptance _____

_____

2. Statement of self-criticism _____

_____

   Statement of self-love and acceptance _____

_____

Use this space to reflect on the above experience of practicing a different response to self-criticism.

_____

_____

_____

_____

_____

_____

Guided Journaling for Nellie's Message 1:

"Shower with one minute of self-love and acceptance daily."

What did you discover or re-discover in this section about *self-love and acceptance*?

_____

_____

_____

How might you put those discoveries into action to replenish yourself?

_____

_____

_____

How can replenishing yourself with deliberately created intentions support you in nurturing others?

_____

_____

_____

_____

If you choose to put this message about self-love and acceptance into action, the following pages are for you to journal your experiences along the way. There are three sets of journaling pages for you to write about three different experiences.

Message 1: Journal of Experiences

What was your experience?

_____

_____

_____

_____

_____

_____

_____

What did you notice about it – before, during, or after?

_____

_____

_____

_____

_____

_____

_____

How has your awareness been raised by this experience?

_____

_____

_____

_____

_____

_____

How can this awareness work for you in other situations?

_____

_____

_____

_____

_____

_____

Message 1: Journal of Experiences

What was your experience?

_____

_____

_____

_____

_____

_____

What did you notice about it – before, during, or after?

_____

_____

_____

_____

_____

_____

How has your awareness been raised by this experience?

_____

_____

_____

_____

_____

_____

_____

How can this awareness work for you in other situations?

_____

_____

_____

_____

_____

_____

_____

Message 1: Journal of Experiences

What was your experience?

_____

_____

_____

_____

_____

_____

What did you notice about it – before, during, or after?

_____

_____

_____

_____

_____

_____

_____

How has your awareness been raised by this experience?

_____

_____

_____

_____

_____

_____

_____

How can this awareness work for you in other situations?

_____

_____

_____

_____

_____

_____

_____

Set simple, well-timed intentions that nurture YOU!

*Intentions are like seeds. When I plant flower seeds
I am confident I'll get flowers, not pumpkins!*
- Nurturing Nellie

For some people the word "intention" is reminiscent of an unkept promise. For Nurturing Nellie, it is quite the opposite. An intention statement declares commitment and focuses our energy on the goal or expectation with confidence that it will be met. Taking a moment or two to deliberately set an intention paves the way for the outcome we desire or expect.

"Watch your language! The words we use can make a huge difference. I used to talk about what I didn't want and expected an automatic positive result. Now I know that when I consciously attend to the result I do want, and articulate that in positive ways, it's like an impulse of energy that gets things moving in the right direction. I keep reminding myself in a light hearted way, "Pay attention to intention!"

Love, Nellie

"Watch your language!" is a playful caveat to call your attention to the words that can inadvertently sabotage your success.

"I don't want to be late for the appointment," *focuses on being late.* Stating what you *don't* want is like planting a pumpkin seed and expecting flowers.

"I intend to get to my appointment on time," *places attention on the positive goal or expectation of being on time.* This statement is not only the positive opposite of the example above, but replaces the word "want" with the word "intend" which is more energizing. It's the flower seed for the flowers we expect.

For even more powerful intention language, let's consider two aspects of intention statements and setting goals: **outer** and **inner**.

The statement *"I intend to get to my appointment on time"* is an example of the **outer aspect** of goal setting.

It's what we're most familiar with: scheduling appointments, planning and accomplishing tasks. This is what we DO and the tangible results we expect to GET. It's the physical level.

The **inner** aspect of goal setting is how we feel and how we "be" when faced with a task, situation, or problem to solve. It's the intangible state of awareness or the spiritual level. I use the verb "be" here with an *active* voice because of its capacity to affect our inner emotional and spiritual state. Remember, we're human "beings" not human "doings" or human "gettings."

Scientific research tells us there is a vibrational frequency or energy associated with our inner attitudes. As you are *doing* or *getting*, how are you *being*? This is the place to nurture yourself - at the inner level of your intention.

"I intend to feel (or "be") relaxed and peaceful" focuses on the inner aspect of our soul or spirit where we can feel gently nurtured.

You can set an intention with an inner aspect or an outer aspect. The new skill here is to combine BOTH aspects. When we set intentions **concurrently** at BOTH the outer level (what we want to accomplish) AND at the inner level (how we want to "be" or feel during the process of accomplishing), we pave the way to successful action by aligning the energy of our thoughts with the energy of our feelings.

The combined intention with both an inner and outer aspect now looks like this:

"I intend to feel relaxed and peaceful as I get to my appointment on time."

In this example, you've just nurtured yourself with some relaxation and peace by trading in scattered or random thoughts for a well-structured intention statement.

The law of attraction tells us we get back the quality of the energy we give out. Be careful! If you don't really have confidence in feeling relaxed and peaceful, your underlying energy of doubt is at play and the words alone might not work. In this case, first imagine yourself in a relaxed and peaceful situation and really "be" that. Then, transfer that feeling to the situation at hand. You can set a well-timed intention for that too: *"I intend to easily transfer this feeling of relaxation to being peaceful and relaxed as I get to my appointment on time."*

"When I learned about intentions, I added two new phrases to my thinking: "like begets like," and "deliberate creation." Flower seeds beget flowers, not pumpkins. If I want to see flowers in my garden, I deliberately plant them, not hope that the seeds might randomly be dropped by a bird! We reap what we sow."

Love, Nellie

Exploring a little further, how does the following statement measure up to declaring a deliberate intention on both the inner and outer levels?

My intention for my visit to the dentist is to be calm, relaxed and grateful for the dentist's expertise to fix my tooth.

My intention for my visit to the dentist is:	**declaration of commitment**
to be calm, relaxed, and grateful for	**inner attitude and energy, calm begets calm**
the dentist's expertise to fix my tooth.	**tangible result expected**

You chose the dentist in whom you have confidence to give you the results you want. Since the result lies with the dentist's expertise and not YOUR expertise, there may be a chance that he or she encounters a problem, needs to do a temporary procedure, and the fix you expected does not happen. Setting an expectation of someone else is tricky. The aspect you set for yourself is still in play. Your demeanor can still be calm and relaxed, even if you need to reschedule another appointment for the final fix with this highly reputable dentist.

Nellie's loving message in action

Setting well-timed intentions throughout the day takes two minutes or less. Choosing specific intentions to write down can make them more concrete, increase the level of commitment and expectation, and amplify the impulse of energy associated with the intention statement.

Ideas for stating intentions

Place a check mark next to the ideas that you might consider using or adapting for your situation. These intentions rely solely on yourself, not on anyone else.

❧ Anytime you transition from one situation to another

• **Upon awakening:**

____ Today my intention is to feel calm and joyful as I deal with a variety of individuals. I intend to approach each person I encounter during the day with kindness.

• **Breakfast: (or any meal)**

____ I intend to focus my attention on easily preparing this meal and enjoy eating it.

• **Coming home, or family comes home to YOU, or you meet friends for lunch/dinner:**

____ I intend to set aside the cares of my day and lovingly greet my family/friends.

• **Upon going to sleep:**

____ I intend to have a peaceful night's sleep and wake up refreshed and fully rested.

❧ When you are faced with a challenge and want to set the tone for a positive outcome

___ Your teenager comes home from school with an unusually low grade on yesterday's algebra test and your signature is required to verify you saw the test. In that moment, before automatically reacting, you can set an intention, such as, **"I intend to stay calm and handle this in a productive way."** In the moment it takes to set the intention to stay calm, you may become aware of a way to proceed peacefully. Instead of stating your opinion or displeasure, perhaps you will be inspired to ask a gentle question, such as "Hmm....I wonder what happened here?"

___ You wrote a report that you spent hours on and your boss calls you in to say she thinks you could have done a better job. Before reacting defensively you set a quick intention, *"I intend to stay composed and be open to hearing her feedback before responding."* Or *"I intend to stay composed, hear her out, and perhaps request time to think about what she's saying before responding."*

❧ When you want to increase the likelihood of an ordinary activity going right

___ I intend to feel relaxed, hopeful, and focused as I eagerly begin to learn this new computer software.

___ My intention is to joyfully and effortlessly let go of the clutter as I clean out this closet. I intend to focus on discerning the usefulness of each item and either keep it, toss it, or pass it along to someone else, with gratitude for having had it when I needed it.

Practice Lovingly – Be gentle with yourself

List a transition, a challenge, and an ordinary activity that you might experience during the week and create an intention statement that can support you on the outer level and nourish you on the inner level.

Transition _____

_____

_____

_____

_____

Challenge _____

_____

_____

_____

_____

Typical Activity _____

_____

_____

_____

_____

Use this space to reflect on the above experience of practicing intention statements.

_____

_____

_____

_____

_____

_____

_____

_____

_____

_____

Guided Journaling for Nellie's Message 2:

"Set simple, well-timed intentions that nurture YOU!"

What did you discover or re-discover in this section about *setting intentions that nurture you?*

_____

_____

_____

How might you put those discoveries into action to replenish yourself?

_____

_____

_____

How can replenishing yourself with deliberately created intentions support you in nurturing others?

_____

_____

_____

_____

If you choose to put this message about setting intentions into action, the following pages are for you to journal your experiences along the way. There are three sets of journaling pages for you to write about three different experiences.

Message 2: Journal of Experiences

What was your experience?

_____

_____

_____

_____

_____

_____

What did you notice about it – before, during, or after?

_____

_____

_____

_____

_____

_____

How has your awareness been raised by this experience?

_____

_____

_____

_____

_____

_____

How can this awareness work for you in other situations?

_____

_____

_____

_____

_____

_____

Message 2: Journal of Experiences

What was your experience?

_____

_____

_____

_____

_____

_____

What did you notice about it – before, during, or after?

_____

_____

_____

_____

_____

_____

How has your awareness been raised by this experience?

_____

_____

_____

_____

_____

_____

_____

How can this awareness work for you in other situations?

_____

_____

_____

_____

_____

_____

_____

Message 2: Journal of Experiences

What was your experience?

_____

_____

_____

_____

_____

_____

_____

What did you notice about it – before, during, or after?

_____

_____

_____

_____

_____

_____

_____

How has your awareness been raised by this experience?

_____

_____

_____

_____

_____

_____

_____

How can this awareness work for you in other situations?

_____

_____

_____

_____

_____

_____

_____

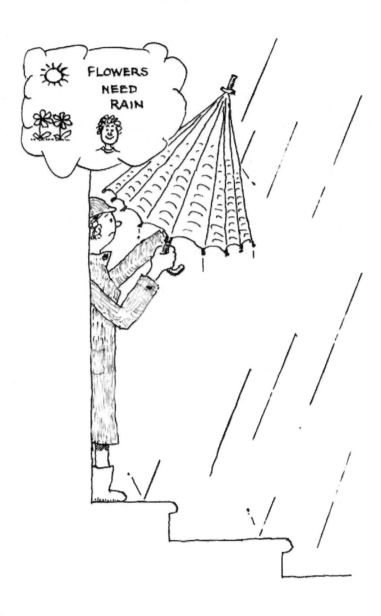

Find inspiration to feed your soul in any given moment

*Rainy days sometimes get me down, so I focus on
picturing the flowers being happy in their moist soil.
To my surprise, the sun appears in the picture and I begin
to smile. I find what I look for, and in the looking
I often uncover hidden inspiration.*
-Nurturing Nellie

Deliberately choosing to look for something is a conscious act. What triggers us to look?

Many answers are obvious: When I misplace my car keys, I look for them. When I lost a watch, I looked for it. I even enjoy using a metal detector when I **haven't** lost anything, purely for the joy of discovering whatever might be hidden under the sand at the beach.

We operate on many levels: physical, mental, emotional and spiritual.

When I am physically missing something I need, I consciously go into action to get it, especially those necessities of life - like food, or an umbrella!

What about other facets of our human condition? What can we do when we are missing something in the mental, emotional, or spiritual realm? What can we do to feed our soul and feel better?

Crossword puzzles, Sudoku and other mental games can fill a void, as can calling a friend for emotional support. Taking a nature walk can lift our spirits. But these require more than a moment or two of our time, and they rely on other people or external resources. Is there another way to look for inspiration without depending on outside sources?

We may remember "daydreaming" as a child, and being strongly coaxed back to reality by a well-meaning adult. Consider choosing to draw upon that age old skill of daydreaming to deliberately nurture your spirit. Using imagination to visualize a positive aspect associated with a seemingly negative situation during a typical day can offer some immediate relief.

As an added bonus, when we let our imagination flow and create something positive in our mind's eye, an unexpected insight, inspiration, or additional positive aspect of the situation often becomes available to us.

Notice the definitions of the word **inspiration** at the intangible level of mind or spirit, and at the physical level of our body.

The Random House Webster's College Dictionary, 2001, lists several entries for the word **inspiration**, two of them are:

"**Entry 5**. *Theol.* a divine influence directly and immediately exerted upon the mind or soul.

Entry 6. the drawing of air into the lungs; inhalation."

"I used to think that **wanting to feel better** mentally, emotionally, or spiritually in any given moment was a luxury for which I had no time to take action during my typically busy day. Just keep "doing" whatever I'm doing, I thought, the results are what's important. I can take a walk later, and later never came.

True, results may be important, yet nurturing myself while I'm working on a task is also important.

I learned that feeling better in any given moment could be accomplished by just noticing the contrast, and using it to make a shift. How do I feel, how would I rather feel?

Since there's usually no time to go out into nature, or turn to a cross-word puzzle in the demands of a busy day, I began to find inner ways to feel better in the very moment I noticed the contrast.

One way I find relief is by consciously focusing on my breathing for a moment; quieting my mind to experience a simple positive shift in how I feel. I often notice that in the quiet moment of simple meditation I am influenced by a thought or idea - a hidden gift that seems to have come from a divine power or from my own soul's inner guidance."

Love, Nellie

Nellie's loving message in action

We often notice contrasts throughout our day, but fail to act for a variety of reasons. Let the contrast - the difference between how you feel and how you'd rather feel - be the trigger, then choose the appropriate action. Do you want to shift gears and nurture yourself for a few minutes, or is it best to continue your activity? Each situation may call for a different answer.

Deliberately choosing to find inspiration takes less than five minutes. With practice, it can become a regular part of daily living.

Focusing on breathing or using imagination may not always result in Divine inspiration. We can find "earthly" inspiration by asking a simple question that can help us shift into better spirits:

What's the best thing I can do for myself right now?

The answers might be:

- ☑ Set an intention that nurtures YOU (See Message 2)
- ☑ Shower with one minute of acceptance and self-love (See Message 1)
- ☑ Take five minutes to clear the chatter in your mind, focus on your breath. Guide yourself through a simple breathing meditation – *breathing in calm, breathing out tension; breathing in lightness, breathing out burdens; breathing in peace, breathing out turmoil.*

More ideas:

- ☑ Visualize yourself taking a walk in nature
- ☑ Sing or hum a comforting song
- ☑ Laugh out loud!
- ☑ Smile for 30 seconds
- ☑ State how you'd rather feel and visualize yourself in that state of being. Daydream for two or three minutes and use your imagination to create your ideal situation in your mind's eye.

The above possibilities require no budget increase, no electronic device for music, no external resources. YOU are the resource that's always available to you!

Practice Lovingly – Be gentle with yourself

Deliberately look for inspiration and expect to find some!
What are 3 ways you might find inspiration in any given moment?

1 _____

2 _____

3 _____

Use this space to reflect on the following question:

What is valuable for you about "finding inspiration in any given moment" as a regular skill in your daily life?

_____

_____

_____

_____

_____

_____

_____

Guided Journaling for Nellie's Message 3:

"Find inspiration to feed your soul in any given moment."

What did you discover or re-discover in this section about *finding inspiration in any given moment?*

_____

_____

_____

How might you put those discoveries into action to replenish yourself?

_____

_____

_____

How can replenishing yourself with deliberately created intentions support you in nurturing others?

_____

_____

_____

_____

If you choose to put this message about finding inspiration into action, the following pages are for you to journal your experiences along the way. There are three sets of journaling pages for you to write about three different experiences.

Message 3: Journal of Experiences

What was your experience?

_____

_____

_____

_____

_____

_____

_____

What did you notice about it – before, during, or after?

_____

_____

_____

_____

_____

_____

_____

How has your awareness been raised by this experience?

_____

_____

_____

_____

_____

_____

_____

How can this awareness work for you in other situations?

_____

_____

_____

_____

_____

_____

_____

Message 3: Journal of Experiences

What was your experience?

_____

_____

_____

_____

_____

_____

What did you notice about it – before, during, or after?

_____

_____

_____

_____

_____

_____

How has your awareness been raised by this experience?

_____

_____

_____

_____

_____

_____

_____

How can this awareness work for you in other situations?

_____

_____

_____

_____

_____

_____

Message 3: Journal of Experiences

What was your experience?

_____

_____

_____

_____

_____

_____

_____

What did you notice about it – before, during, or after?

_____

_____

_____

_____

_____

_____

_____

How has your awareness been raised by this experience?

_____

_____

_____

_____

_____

_____

_____

How can this awareness work for you in other situations?

_____

_____

_____

_____

_____

_____

_____

Replace multi-tasking with mindfulness

I used to think multi-tasking was a virtue.
Now I'm more aware of focusing my attention on
one thing at a time, and I feel so much better.
Focused attention brings life to daily living.
-Nurturing Nellie

When I hear the word mindfulness, I think of its opposite — especially paired with the word *eating*. *"Mindless eating"* conjures up images of folks at a movie theater with huge buckets of popcorn, raising hand to mouth unconsciously as they focus on the big screen. I wonder how much they really notice the flavor and crunchiness of those popped kernels after the first few moments.

I remember a sign I saw on a visit to England. The stairway of the old building was narrow, and as I descended, I noticed that the height of the doorway at the bottom of the stair was less than six feet. As an American I was amused with the warning above the door, "Mind your head!" But it makes perfect sense, and certainly heightened my awareness about the height of the door!

These two scenarios give us a glimpse into mindfulness: noticing, awareness, consciousness, focused attention, being in the moment.

"Mindfulness requires being alert, putting energy into the current moment, and using all of your senses to be present. I once took part in an exercise where we used all of our senses to focus on eating a single raisin. The leader's voice guided us - in slow motion - to look at the raisin in our hand, feel it, smell it, place it on our tongue, move it around, hear any sound as we gently bit into it, focus on flavor, texture, while chewing, and all the while, just noticing whatever we noticed with our senses. I always thought of raisins as dried fruit and this time I noticed how juicy a raisin is. What I didn't focus on during the exercise was the argument with my friend the day before or the bill I had to pay the next day. There was no stress. Ahh, it felt so good to be focused on just one thing."

Love, Nellie

Nellie's loving message in action

Deliberately focusing our attention throughout the day takes NO EXTRA TIME and can leave us feeling refreshed by clearing out the chatter in our heads, and enjoying all aspects of what we're doing: seeing, hearing, smelling, tasting, touching, or feeling emotionally. Focusing mindfully can obviously save us from simple mishaps or serious accidents and it is a simple way to release our stressful thoughts by replacing them with the energy of the moment.

Noticing all the attributes of what we're focused on can enrich the experience of daily life.

When is a good time to use mindfulness?

❧ Any time! Focused attention is a gift to give yourself. It brings life to daily living.

❧ Mindfulness can even SAVE us time. How often do we have to re-do something because we weren't focused on doing it right the first time?

Ideas for focusing attention and being in the now

Mark the ideas you might consider using or adapting to your situation:

_____ Upon going to sleep: Notice how warm and comfortable your pillow is. Notice the smell of fresh linens on the bed.

_____ Upon awakening: Notice the beautiful sunlight creeping through the window. Do you hear any birds? Do you hear the sounds of the city waking up?

_____ When you water a plant take a different point of view and look at the under side of the leaves. Listen to the water as it meets the soil. Watch the soil interact with the water. Does it soak it up, or is the water sitting on top for awhile?

_____ Release nagging worries about a problem by designating time to work on solving it. When the time arrives be in the moment as you look at the possibilities, the realities, and the vision for solving the problem. Work on it for five minutes, 15 minutes, or an hour if that's what it takes - perhaps in the presence of a professional who can lay out additional options. Consciously focus on all aspects of the solution and the process of creating the solution. Then get up, move on, and focus on the next task. Whew! Can it be that easy? Setting an intention at the inner and outer levels can help with this one. **"I intend to easily release this worry about writing my resume and designate one hour to joyfully handle it on Thursday after supper."** Refer to Message 2 for more about intention statements.

Practice Lovingly – Be gentle with yourself

What is valuable for you about using mindfulness and focusing full attention on:

Drinking a cup of coffee or tea

_____

Eating or preparing food

_____

Listening to your kids, family, friends, co-workers

_____

_____

Solving problems

_____

_____

Handling tasks or activities

List a few specific tasks:

_____

_____

_____

_____

Guided Journaling for Nellie's Message 4:

"Replace multi-tasking with mindfulness"

What did you discover or re-discover in this section about focused attention, being in the moment, or mindfulness?

_____

_____

_____

How might you put those discoveries into action to replenish yourself?

_____

_____

_____

How can replenishing yourself with mindfulness support you in nurturing others?

_____

_____

_____

_____

If you choose to put this message about focused attention and mindfulness into action, the following pages are for you to journal your experiences along the way. There are three sets of journaling pages for you to write about three different experiences.

Message 4: Journal of Experiences

What was your experience?

_____

_____

_____

_____

_____

_____

_____

What did you notice about it – before, during, or after?

_____

_____

_____

_____

_____

_____

_____

How has your awareness been raised by this experience?

_____

_____

_____

_____

_____

_____

_____

How can this awareness work for you in other situations?

_____

_____

_____

_____

_____

_____

_____

Message 4: Journal of Experiences

What was your experience?

_____

_____

_____

_____

_____

_____

What did you notice about it – before, during, or after?

_____

_____

_____

_____

_____

_____

How has your awareness been raised by this experience?

_____

_____

_____

_____

_____

_____

_____

How can this awareness work for you in other situations?

_____

_____

_____

_____

_____

_____

Message 4: Journal of Experiences

What was your experience?

_____

_____

_____

_____

_____

_____

What did you notice about it – before, during, or after?

_____

_____

_____

_____

_____

_____

How has your awareness been raised by this experience?

_____

_____

_____

_____

_____

_____

How can this awareness work for you in other situations?

_____

_____

_____

_____

_____

_____

Document your attitude of gratitude as a gift to yourself

Gratitude and appreciation are expressions of joy.
When I deliberately appreciate the blessings in my life,
I create more joy in myself.
-Nurturing Nellie

"Count your blessings" is an old saying worth renewing.

What if you opened a "gratitude bank account" and made a deposit several times a day of all the things you appreciate? How quickly would you accumulate an abundance of joy from all of your blessings?

Blessings come in many shapes and sizes. Some are material gifts for which we send a note of appreciation. There are also gifts of the heart, like a compliment, that we readily acknowledge and appreciate with a simple "thank you." Some are gifts of nature like fresh air, sunshine, rain, and beautiful flowers. Others are gifts of insight, wisdom, or learning.

When we are open to recognizing the positive aspects of our surroundings and events in daily life we can notice many more simple things to be grateful for that can nurture our soul – a soft pillow, an alarm clock that keeps us on schedule, indoor plumbing! Imagine what life was like when people ventured outdoors in freezing temperatures to use the outhouse!

*"I am grateful for being open to new ideas and re-discovering old ones. I appreciate the books and teachers who have inspired me to grow and stretch myself to new levels of awareness. I now know that the phrase "**we reap what we sow**" refers not only to deeds, but also to thoughts and words. So when I am expressing gratitude for a blessing in my life, it's like planting a seed to grow more of the same. And I do!"*

Love, Nellie

Nellie's loving message in action

Noticing an obvious blessing for which to be thankful takes less than a minute. Stating the thanks quietly can happen simultaneously.

Deliberately choosing to find something to appreciate takes less than five minutes, and with practice, can become a regular part of daily living.

Practice Lovingly – Be gentle with yourself

☑ Begin to notice the positive aspects of a situation. Some are obvious. Some can be found by deliberately seeking. What's positive for a woman who just lost her job? It might be that she really wanted to work in a different environment but was afraid to give up the secure paycheck for the unknown. Or, it could be that through vigorous networking to find employment she makes connections that take her beyond what she might have hoped for.

☑ Become aware of positive evidence that life is supporting you and your desires. An example of positive evidence is: you might be struggling to find a solution to a problem and happen to turn on the radio just in time to hear someone offering a resource related to that very issue. What many people call a favorable "coincidence" can be considered as evidence that "life is out to do me good."

☑ Make deposits of appreciation, blessings, and positive evidence as often as you can, first by verbally acknowledging them, then following up with and entry in your gratitude journal. The second part of this book is designed as a journal to make "deposits" in your "gratitude bank account."

"Reap the rewards of what you sow!

Your gratitude bank yields a high return on your investment of time and effort in making "deposits."

The abundance in the gratitude bank can be used to balance out times when you might be experiencing difficulty or just feeling a bit down – and you don't have to make a withdrawal! The high energy of gratitude and appreciation is permanently entered in your account and available 24/7 for you to access simply by reviewing the contents. Reading the list quietly is uplifting. Try reading it out loud and notice your energy amping up another notch."

Love, Nellie

When is a good time to make a deposit in my gratitude bank account?

Anytime you notice a positive aspect about a situation, a blessing, or positive evidence that life is out to do you good, acknowledge it in your heart and mind. Expressing your appreciation in that moment, quietly or aloud, is energizing, joyful, and can bring you a perspective that nurtures you to stay centered or grounded amidst turmoil or disorder.

Ideas for documenting your attitude of gratitude

Some people like to keep a small notebook with them and write entries or "deposits" during the day. Taking time at lunch to document gratitude is a way to nurture yourself with some spiritual balance amidst a busy work day. This book is sized specifically so that you can keep it handy and use the gratitude journal often.

Journaling your gratitude in the evening as you begin to unwind and prepare for a restful night's sleep can be very nurturing. Remembering the many blessings from the day can be calming and uplifting.

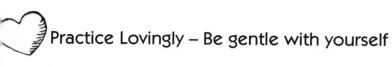 **Practice Lovingly – Be gentle with yourself**

What is valuable for you about acknowledging blessings and keeping a "gratitude bank account" as a regular principle in your daily life?

_____

_____

_____

_____

_____

_____

_____

_____

_____

Guided Journaling for Message 5 from Nurturing Nellie:

"Document your attitude of gratitude."

What did you discover or re-discover in this section on appreciation and gratitude?

_____

_____

_____

How might you put those discoveries into action to replenish yourself?

_____

_____

_____

How can replenishing yourself through gratitude and appreciation
support you in nurturing OTHERS?

_____

_____

_____

If you choose to put this message about acknowledging
blessings and keeping a gratitude bank account into action,
the following pages are for you to journal your experiences
as you go along. There are three sets of journaling pages for you to
write about three different experiences.

Message 5: Journal of Experiences

What was your experience?

_____

_____

_____

_____

_____

_____

What did you notice about it – before, during, or after?

_____

_____

_____

_____

_____

_____

How has your awareness been raised by this experience?

_____

_____

_____

_____

_____

_____

_____

How can this awareness work for you in other situations?

_____

_____

_____

_____

_____

_____

Message 5: Journal of Experiences

What was your experience?

_____

_____

_____

_____

_____

_____

What did you notice about it – before, during, or after?

_____

_____

_____

_____

_____

_____

How has your awareness been raised by this experience?

_____

_____

_____

_____

_____

_____

_____

How can this awareness work for you in other situations?

_____

_____

_____

_____

_____

_____

_____

Message 5: Journal of Experiences

What was your experience?

_____

_____

_____

_____

_____

_____

What did you notice about it – before, during, or after?

_____

_____

_____

_____

_____

_____

How has your awareness been raised by this experience?

_____

_____

_____

_____

_____

_____

_____

How can this awareness work for you in other situations?

_____

_____

_____

_____

_____

_____

_____

Continue the nurturing

Yes! We need to take time for ourselves to replenish body, mind and spirit.

Nurturing Nellie is my way of reminding women that it's not only okay to be the recipient of self-care, self-love and self-nurturing, it is essential to our well-being and spirit of compassion as we live the words "Love thy neighbor as thyself." We bring out our best, and we honor others with gifts of love, time and energy, when we first have those gifts available to ourselves.

What's valuable about Nellie's messages is that they are geared toward shifting our thinking to increase energy and personal well-being in simple daily situations without needing to schedule additional time to do so.

When you cultivate the soil, plant flower seeds, and nurture them with water and sunlight you are able to enjoy the magnificence of a beautiful floral bouquet.

I hope you have enjoyed Nellie's messages and will continue to discover additional ways to gently replenish yourself, and enjoy the magnificence of your own bouquet of self-love, self-care and self-nurturing, as you joyfully offer love, care and kindness to others.

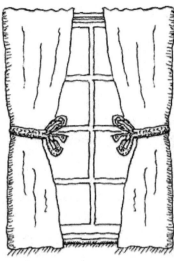

BOOK
OF
GRATITUDE
This book
belongs to

MY
BLESSINGS

Count Your Blessings Gratitude Journal

"The following pages are for you to keep track of the abundance in your life as good things accumulate over time.

You may want to consider this your "gratitude bank account" and enter "deposits" in the form of:

- ☑ Gratitude for blessings and inspiration in your life
- ☑ Material things you are thankful for
- ☑ Gifts of the heart, such as a compliment or a "thinking of you" note
- ☑ Aspects of nature that you consider a blessing or a gift
- ☑ Insights, learning, self-discovery or wisdom that you acquire
- ☑ Positive aspects associated with ordinary negative situations
- ☑ Positive outcomes that arise out of a challenging circumstance
- ☑ Positive evidence that life is supporting you along your journey

Consider several ways to make this joyful for YOU.
Write in list form, phrases, sentences, paragraphs…
any format that feels good for you at the time.
For added fun - sketches, cartoons and doodles
are highly recommended,
as is writing with colored pens. Enjoy!"

Love, Nellie

Date _____

Date _____

_____

_____

_____

_____

_____

_____

_____

_____

_____

_____

_____

_____

_____

_____

_____

_____

_____

_____

Date _____

Date _____

Date _____

_____

_____

_____

_____

_____

_____

_____

_____

_____

_____

_____

_____

_____

_____

_____

_____

_____

_____

Date _____

_____
_____
_____
_____
_____
_____
_____
_____
_____
_____
_____
_____
_____
_____
_____
_____
_____
_____
_____
_____

Date _____

Date _____

_____

_____

_____

_____

_____

_____

_____

_____

_____

_____

_____

_____

_____

_____

_____

_____

Date _____

Date _____

_____

_____

_____

_____

_____

_____

_____

_____

_____

_____

_____

_____

_____

_____

_____

_____

_____

Date _____

Date _____

_____

_____

_____

_____

_____

_____

_____

_____

_____

_____

_____

_____

_____

_____

_____

_____

_____

_____

Date _____

_____
_____
_____
_____
_____
_____
_____
_____
_____
_____
_____
_____
_____
_____
_____
_____
_____
_____
_____
_____
_____
_____

Date _____

_____

_____

_____

_____

_____

_____

_____

_____

_____

_____

_____

_____

_____

_____

_____

_____

_____

_____

_____

_____

Date _____

_____

_____

_____

_____

_____

_____

_____

_____

_____

_____

_____

_____

_____

_____

_____

_____

_____

Date _____

_____
_____
_____
_____
_____
_____
_____
_____
_____
_____
_____
_____
_____
_____
_____
_____
_____

Date _____

Date _____

_____

_____

_____

_____

_____

_____

_____

_____

_____

_____

_____

_____

_____

_____

_____

_____

_____

_____

_____

_____

Date _____

_____

_____

_____

_____

_____

_____

_____

_____

_____

_____

_____

_____

_____

_____

_____

_____

Date _____

Date _____

_____

_____

_____

_____

_____

_____

_____

_____

_____

_____

_____

_____

_____

_____

_____

_____

_____

_____

_____

Date _____

_____
_____
_____
_____
_____
_____
_____
_____
_____
_____
_____
_____
_____
_____
_____
_____
_____
_____
_____
_____

Date _____

_____

_____

_____

_____

_____

_____

_____

_____

_____

_____

_____

_____

_____

_____

_____

_____

_____

Date _____

_____
_____
_____
_____
_____
_____
_____
_____
_____
_____
_____
_____
_____
_____
_____
_____
_____
_____
_____

Date _____

Date _____

_____
_____
_____
_____
_____
_____
_____
_____
_____
_____
_____
_____
_____
_____
_____
_____
_____
_____
_____

Date _____

Date _____

_____

_____

_____

_____

_____

_____

_____

_____

_____

_____

_____

_____

_____

_____

_____

_____

_____

_____

_____

_____

_____

Date _____

_____

_____

_____

_____

_____

_____

_____

_____

_____

_____

_____

_____

_____

_____

_____

_____

_____

_____

Date _____

_____
_____
_____
_____
_____
_____
_____
_____
_____
_____
_____
_____
_____
_____
_____
_____
_____
_____
_____
_____

Date _____

_____

_____

_____

_____

_____

_____

_____

_____

_____

_____

_____

_____

_____

_____

_____

_____

_____

Date _____

_____
_____
_____
_____
_____
_____
_____
_____
_____
_____
_____
_____
_____
_____
_____
_____
_____
_____
_____

Date _____

_____

_____

_____

_____

_____

_____

_____

_____

_____

_____

_____

_____

_____

_____

_____

_____

_____

Date _____

_____

_____

_____

_____

_____

_____

_____

_____

_____

_____

_____

_____

_____

_____

_____

_____

_____

_____

Date _____

Date _____

_____
_____
_____
_____
_____
_____
_____
_____
_____
_____
_____
_____
_____
_____
_____
_____
_____
_____
_____

Date _____

Date _____

Bibliography

A note from the author:

The following books have had an influence on my personal journey, professional work, and writing. Readers of this book may enjoy exploring works of the authors listed below.

Rhonda Byrne — **The Secret**

Deepak Chopra, M.D. — **Creating Affluence**
Wealth Consciousness in the Field of All Possibilities

Wayne W. Dyer — **There's A Spiritual Solution to Every Problem**

Wayne W. Dyer — **Your Sacred Self**
Making the Decision to Be Free

Dave Ellis — **Becoming A Master Student**

Dave Ellis and Stan Lankowitz — **Human Being**

Adele Faber And Elaine Mazlish — **How to Talk So Kids Will Listen and Listen So Kids Will Talk**

David R. Hawkins, M.D., Ph.D. — **Power vs. Force**
The Hidden Determinants of Human Behavior

Louise L. Hay — **You Can Heal Your Life**

Esther and Jerry Hicks — **Ask and It Is Given**
Learning to Manifest Your Desires

Ernest Holmes

The Science of Mind
A Philosophy, A Faith, A Way of Life

Michael J Losier

Law of Attraction
The Science of Attracting More of What You
Want and Less of What You Don't

Jim Loehr and
Tony Schwartz

The Power of Full Engagement
Managing Energy, Not Time, Is the Key to
High Performance and Personal Renewal

Bruce Mc Arthur

Your Life
Why It Is the Way It Is and What You Can Do
About It

Eckhart Tolle

The Power of Now
A Guide to Spiritual Enlightenment

Eckhart Tolle

A New Earth
Awakening To Your Life's Purpose

Doreen Virtue, Ph.D.

Divine Guidance
How To Have A Dialogue With God and
Your Guardian Angels

CPSIA information can be obtained at www.ICGtesting.com
Printed in the USA
BVOW09s2105031114

373090BV00003B/4/P